This
Whitaker Playhouse
Book Belongs To:

_____

In Him was life; and the life was the light of men.

John 1:4

THE STORY OF EASTER
www.philsmouse.com
ISBN: 978-1-64123-619-5
© 2021 by Phil A. Smouse

Whitaker House
1030 Hunt Valley Circle
New Kensington, PA 15068
www.whitakerhouse.com

The Story of Easter

A Note to Parents...

Your word is a lamp to my feet, and a light to my path. Psalm 119:105

if you love the wonderful, rollicking rhythm and rhyme of the classic picture books you read as a child and want to bring that same sense of joy to your children, you're in the right place.

Learning, understanding, and living God's Word is a journey that lasts a lifetime. And that journey starts by reading God's Word. Every tiny heart on the face of this earth is trying to find its way home to Jesus. And God's eternal promise to our precious little lambs is that they will find Him—when we take the time to show them how and where to look.

Jesus wants us to be His—one hundred percent. And the most important thing is not what we say or do, or even who we reach. The most important thing is the relationship we cultivate with Him.

That deep spiritual connection isn't only for adults. The truths you share with your children from God's Word will stay with them for the rest of their lives. This delightful, child-friendly Bible story is a perfect way to introduce those precious little ones to the joy of a heart filled with Jesus and the knowledge of God's Word.

Phil A. Smouse

I am the way, the truth,
and the life.
John 14:6

i saw it ALL!

Yes, I was there.
You say, *"no way,"* but *au contraire!*
Two guys walked up from you-know-where,
and said, *"Untie those two right there!"*

"Those two right there?" our master plead.
They nodded, "Yes!" then boldly said,
"The Lord our God has need of them.
We're going to Jerusalem!"

"*Jerusalem?*" we softly said.
"That's right!" they smiled
and off we sped!

They scrubbed us up with soap and suds,
put on our finest donkey-duds,
then buffed and polished, plucked and picked,
until we both were smooth and slicked.

"*Hee-haw!*" Two friends, genteel and dressed,
both decked out in our Sunday best.
Two hearts alive with wonderous things,
sent off to see the King of Kings!

And as those two bold, godly guys
knelt down and prayed, to my surprise,
He called *MY name* with loving care,
as people came from *everywhere!*

They took their hats and coats and robes,
their frocks and gowns, their caps and clothes,
and threw them down into the street,
right underneath my fumbly feet!

A million people, maybe more,
squeezed into every house and store,
as every roof and porch and gutter,
filled with joy, began to utter,

"Bless'd is He who comes this day!
The Son of David! Christ! The way!
The Son of God! Our Savior brings,
Hosanna! Jesus! King of Kings!"

We clopped on through the multitude,
as every damsel, dapper-dude,
old gravely grandma, gramp and Gus
palm-branched the road in front of us.

The temple gates swung open wide,
and, oh what Jesus saw inside!
His big, brown eyes popped halfway out,
then He began to twist and shout!

"God's house should be a house of prayer,
but look what you've done over there,
and over here and under those!"
His godly anger rose and rose.

He grabbed a whip and whipped it good!
He cleaned up just the way you should.
He turned their tables, smashed their lies,
swept out the mean and naughty guys,
who loved to rob good godly folk,
until their godly lives were broke.

Some people shouted, *"Praise the Lord!"*
But others whispered, "This means war!"

Those fine, religious folks were hot.
Their fine religious world was shot!
If Jesus *was* the Son of God,
then *they* were nothing but a fraud!

So all week long, each night and day,
they tried and tried to find a way
to kill God's one and only Son,
if not for spite than just for fun.

And just that quick, yes just like that,
as Jesus and His friends all sat
for one last supper, Jesus knew
what those religious guys would do!

They wined and dined, then off they crept
down to the garden, *where they slept*,
as Jesus prayed and prayed and prayed.
The time had come. He'd been betrayed!

The elders grinned an evil grin.
They hauled Him up and tossed Him in!
They barked and howled, guffawed and fought,
(unlike God's Ten Commandments taught!)

Did Jesus shout for His release?
No! Like a lamb, *He held His peace.*
The High Priest gawked and then arose,
and tore his fine religious clothes!

The Roman leaders got Him next,
but Pontius Pilate was perplexed.
"Behold the Man! The King of Kings?
The Man accused of many things!"

The crowd was mad! At what or who?
No one could say. Nobody knew!
"What shall I do, then?" Pilate swore.
"Crucify Him," they all roared!

And so they nailed Him to the cross.
Our hearts were torn. Our hope was lost.
But as He hung and bled and died. . .

"Father, forgive them!" Jesus cried.

They laid Him in a cold, dark room,
then rolled a stone to seal His tomb.
"Who was this man?" a soldier cried,
"Who lived and loved and bled and died,
to free us from our life of sin,
and save us to be born – *again?"*

The lightning flashed.
The thunder boomed.
The temple veil was torn in two!
Darkness. Silence. *"Why, oh why?"*
Our desperate, broken hearts all cried.

But three days later, He arose.
Alive again! For heaven knows,
and all the earth can shout and sing
that Jesus IS the King of Kings!
Yes, God's most precious work of art,
alive right here inside my heart!

No man comes to the Father, but by Me.

John 14:6

There's still more fun from Whitaker Playhouse.

My Big Book of Bible Stories
978-1-64123-548-8

From award-winning author and illustrator Phil A. Smouse, *My Big Book of Bible Stories* features seventeen favorite Bible stories told in hilarious rhymes, with bright, full-color illustrations. These clever retellings of key Scriptures from the Old and New Testaments include the stories of creation, Adam and Eve, Jonah, the Good Samaritan, Jesus and Nicodemus, Peter, and more. Parents will enjoy reading *My Big Book of Bible Stories* to their preschool children, while young readers will delight in the whimsical story-telling and artwork.

My Big Book of Bible People, Places, and Things
978-1-64123-549-5

This brand-new Bible dictionary for kids features 750 entries with witty, age-appropriate text and colorful illustrations from award-winning author and illustrator Phil A. Smouse. *My Big Book of Bible People, Places, and Things* explains important terms in simple ways that young readers can easily grasp, while the full-color illustrations enhance your child's learning. With such entries as "Alleluia," "Book of Life," "Mary and Martha," and "Walking on Water," this book provides an important head start to scriptural literacy.

Bible ABCs   978-1-64123-428-3

Bible Activities   978-1-64123-430-6

Noah's Animals   978-1-64123-429-0

Bible 123s   978-1-64123-427-6

Away in a Manger   978-1-64123-527-3

Merry Christmas   978-1-64123-528-0

Wipe-Clean Activity Books

The *Inspired to Learn* series from Whitaker Playhouse is a perfect way for parents to share God's love with children while also introducing early learning concepts in a fun, interactive way.

These durable, wipe-clean books will provide hours of entertainment as children learn counting, the alphabet, color and shape recognition, drawing, spotting differences, and more. Parents will delight in their little one's progress as they enjoy the creative exercises.